Piano • Vocal

Walt Disney Pictures Presents

THE LION KING

ORIGINAL SONGS
MUSIC *by* ELTON JOHN
LYRICS *by* TIM RICE

4	CIRCLE OF LIFE
14	I JUST CAN'T WAIT TO BE KING
22	BE PREPARED
32	HAKUNA MATATA
42	CAN YOU FEEL THE LOVE TONIGHT
48	LYRICS
56	CAN YOU FEEL THE LOVE TONIGHT As Performed by ELTON JOHN
60	CIRCLE OF LIFE As Performed by ELTON JOHN
66	I JUST CAN'T WAIT TO BE KING As Performed by ELTON JOHN

ISBN 0-7935-3416-X

Artwork © The Walt Disney Company

7777 W. BLUEMOUND RD. P.O. BOX 13819 MILWAUKEE, WI 53213

Copyright ©1994 by HAL LEONARD CORPORATION
International Copyright Secured   All Rights Reserved

For all works contained herein:
Unauthorized copying, arranging, adapting, recording or public performance is an infringement of copyright.
Infringers are liable under the law.

CIRCLE OF LIFE

Music by ELTON JOHN
Lyrics by TIM RICE

© 1994 Wonderland Music Company, Inc.
International Copyright Secured   All Rights Reserved

CIRCLE OF LIFE

Music *by* Elton John
Lyrics *by* Tim Rice

From the day we arrive on the planet
And blinking, step into the sun
There's more to see than can ever be seen
More to do than can ever be done
There's far too much to take in here
More to find than can ever be found
But the sun rolling high
Through the sapphire sky
Keeps great and small on the endless round

*It's the circle of life
And it moves us all
Through despair and hope
Through faith and love
Till we find our place
On the path unwinding
In the circle
The circle of life*

*It's the circle of life
And it moves us all
Through despair and hope
Through faith and love
Till we find our place
On the path unwinding
In the circle
The circle of life*

© 1994 Wonderland Music Company, Inc.
International Copyright Secured   All Rights Reserved

CIRCLE OF LIFE

As Performed *by* Elton John
Music *by* Elton John
Lyrics *by* Tim Rice

From the day we arrive on the planet
And blinking, step into the sun
There's more to be seen than can ever be seen
More to do than can ever be done

Some say eat or be eaten
Some say live and let live
But all are agreed as they join the stampede
You should never take more than you give

Chorus
In the circle of life
It's the wheel of fortune
It's the leap of faith
It's the band of hope
Till we find our place
On the path unwinding
In the circle, in the circle of life

Some of us fall by the wayside
And some of us soar to the stars
And some of us sail through our troubles
And some have to live with the scars

There's far too much to take in here
More to find than can ever be found
But the sun rolling high
Through the sapphire sky
Keeps great and small on the endless round

Chorus repeats

© 1994 Wonderland Music Company, Inc.
International Copyright Secured   All Rights Reserved

I JUST CAN'T WAIT TO BE KING

Music by Elton John
Lyrics by Tim Rice

I'm gonna be a mighty king
So enemies beware!

Well, I've never seen a king of beasts
With quite so little hair

I'm gonna be the mane event
Like no king was before
I'm brushing up on looking down
I'm working on my roar

Thus far, a rather uninspiring thing

Oh, I just can't wait to be king!

No one saying do this
No one saying be there
No one saying stop that
No one saying see here
Free to run around all day
Free to do it all my way

I think it's time that you and I
Arranged a heart to heart

Kings don't need advice
From little hornbills for a start
If this is where the monarchy is headed
Count me out
Out of service, out of Africa
I wouldn't hang about

This child is getting wildly out of wing

Oh, I just can't wait to be king!

Everybody look left
Everybody look right
Everywhere you look I'm
Standing in the spotlight

Let every creature go for broke and sing
Let's hear it in the herd and on the wing
It's gonna be King Simba's finest fling

Oh, I just can't wait to be king!
Oh, I just can't wait to be king!
Oh, I just can't wait to be king!

© 1994 Wonderland Music Company, Inc.
International Copyright Secured   All Rights Reserved

I JUST CAN'T WAIT TO BE KING

As Performed *by* **Elton John**
Music by Elton John
Lyrics by Tim Rice

Way beyond the water hole
A little down the line
The jungle and the plains and peaks
Are scheduled to be mine

I'm gonna be the ruler
Of most everything around
From the grandest of the mountains
To the humble common ground
My reign will be a super-awesome thing
Oh, I just can't wait to be king

I'm gonna be a noble king
So enemies beware!
I only need a little time
Perhaps a little hair

I'm gonna be the mane event
Like no king was before
I'm brushing up on looking down
I'm working on my roar
The fauna and the flora gonna swing
Oh, I just can't wait to be king

Chorus
*No one saying do this
No one saying be there
No one saying stop that
No one saying see here
Free to run around all day
I'll be free to do it my way*

*No one saying do this
No one saying be there
No one saying stop that
No one saying see here
Free to run around all day
Free to do it my way*

The time has come
As someone said
To talk of many things
This may be true
But I would rather stick to talking kings

It's easy to be royal
If you're already leonine
It isn't just my right
Even my left will be divine
The monarchy is waiting to go zing
Oh, I just can't wait to be king

Oh, I just can't wait to be king
(Repeat until fade)

© 1994 Wonderland Music Company, Inc.
International Copyright Secured   All Rights Reserved

BE PREPARED

Music by Elton John
Lyrics by Tim Rice

I know that your powers of retention
Are as wet as a warthog's backside
But thick as you are, pay attention
My words are a matter of pride

It's clear from your vacant expressions
The lights are not all on upstairs
But we're talking kings and successions
Even you can't be caught unawares

So prepare for a chance of a lifetime
Be prepared for sensational news
A shining new era
Is tiptoeing nearer

And where do we feature?

Just listen to teacher
I know it sounds sordid
But you'll be rewarded
When at last I am given my dues!
And injustice deliciously squared
Be prepared!

It's great that we'll soon be connected
With a king who'll be all-time adored

Of course, quid pro quo, you're expected
To take certain duties on board
The future is littered with prizes
And though I'm the main addressee

The point that I must emphasize is
You won't get a sniff without me

So prepare for the coup of the century
Be prepared for the murkiest scam
(Oooooo, la la la!)
Meticulous planning
(We'll have food!)
Tenacity spanning
(Lots of food)
Decades of denial
(We repeat)
Is simply why I'll
(Endless meat)
Be king undisputed
(Aaaaaaah!)
Respected, saluted
(Aaaaaaah!)
And seen for the wonder I am
(Aaaaaaah!)

Yes, my teeth and ambitions are bared
Be prepared!

Yes, our teeth and ambitions are bared
Be prepared!

© 1994 Wonderland Music Company, Inc.
International Copyright Secured   All Rights Reserved

HAKUNA MATATA

Music by Elton John
Lyrics by Tim Rice

Hakuna Matata!
What a wonderful phrase
Hakuna Matata!
Ain't no passing craze

It means no worries
For the rest of your days
It's our problem-free philosophy
Hakuna Matata!

When he was a young warthog
When I was a young warthog
He found his aroma lacked certain appeal
He could clear the savannah after ev'ry meal
I'm a sensitive soul though I seem thick-skinned
And it hurt that my friends never stood downwind

And, oh, the shame
Thoughta changin' my name
And I got downhearted
Ev'rytime that I…

Hakuna Matata!
What a wonderful phrase
Hakuna Matata!
Ain't no passing craze

It means no worries
For the rest of your days
It's our problem-free philosophy

Hakuna Matata!
(Repeat)

Hakuna…it means no worries
For the rest of your days
It's our problem-free philosophy

Hakuna Matata!
(Repeat)

© 1994 Wonderland Music Company, Inc.
International Copyright Secured   All Rights Reserved

CAN YOU FEEL THE LOVE TONIGHT

Music by Elton John
Lyrics by Tim Rice

I can see what's happ'ning
And they don't have a clue
They'll fall in love and here's the bottom line
Our trio's down to two

The sweet caress of twilight
There's magic everywhere
And with all this romantic atmosphere
Disaster's in the air

Chorus
Can you feel the love tonight?
The peace the evening brings
The world, for once, in perfect harmony
With all its living things

So many things to tell her
But how to make her see
The truth about my past? - Impossible!
She'd turn away from me

He's holding back, he's hiding
But what, I can't decide
Why won't he be the king I know he is
The king I see inside?

Chorus
Can you feel the love tonight?
The peace the evening brings
The world, for once, in perfect harmony
With all its living things

Can you feel the love tonight?
You needn't look too far
Stealing through the night's uncertainties
Love is where they are

And if he falls in love tonight
It can be assumed
His carefree days with us are history
In short, our pal is doomed

© 1994 Wonderland Music Company, Inc.
International Copyright Secured   All Rights Reserved

CAN YOU FEEL THE LOVE TONIGHT

As Performed by Elton John
Music by Elton John
Lyrics by Tim Rice

There's a calm surrender
To the rush of day
When the heat of the rolling world
Can be turned away
An enchanted moment
And it sees me through
It's enough for this restless warrior
Just to be with you

Chorus
And can you feel the love tonight?
It is where we are
It's enough for this wide-eyed wanderer
That we got this far
And can you feel the love tonight
How it's laid to rest?
It's enough to make kings and vagabonds
Believe the very best

There's a time for everyone
If they only learn
That the twisting kaleidoscope
Moves us all in turn
There's a rhyme and reason
To the wild outdoors
When the heart of this star-crossed voyager
Beats in time with yours

Chorus

It's enough to make kings and vagabonds
Believe the very best

© 1994 Wonderland Music Company, Inc.
International Copyright Secured   All Rights Reserved

Can You Feel The Love Tonight
(as performed by ELTON JOHN)

Music by ELTON JOHN
Lyrics by TIM RICE

Pop Ballad

There's a calm surrender to the rush of day, when the heat of the rolling world can be turned away. An enchanted moment,

There's a time for ev-'ry-one, if they only learn that the twisting kaleidoscope moves us all in turn. There's a rhyme and reason

© 1994 Wonderland Music Company, Inc.
International Copyright Secured   All Rights Reserved

CIRCLE OF LIFE
(as performed by ELTON JOHN)

Music by ELTON JOHN
Lyrics by TIM RICE

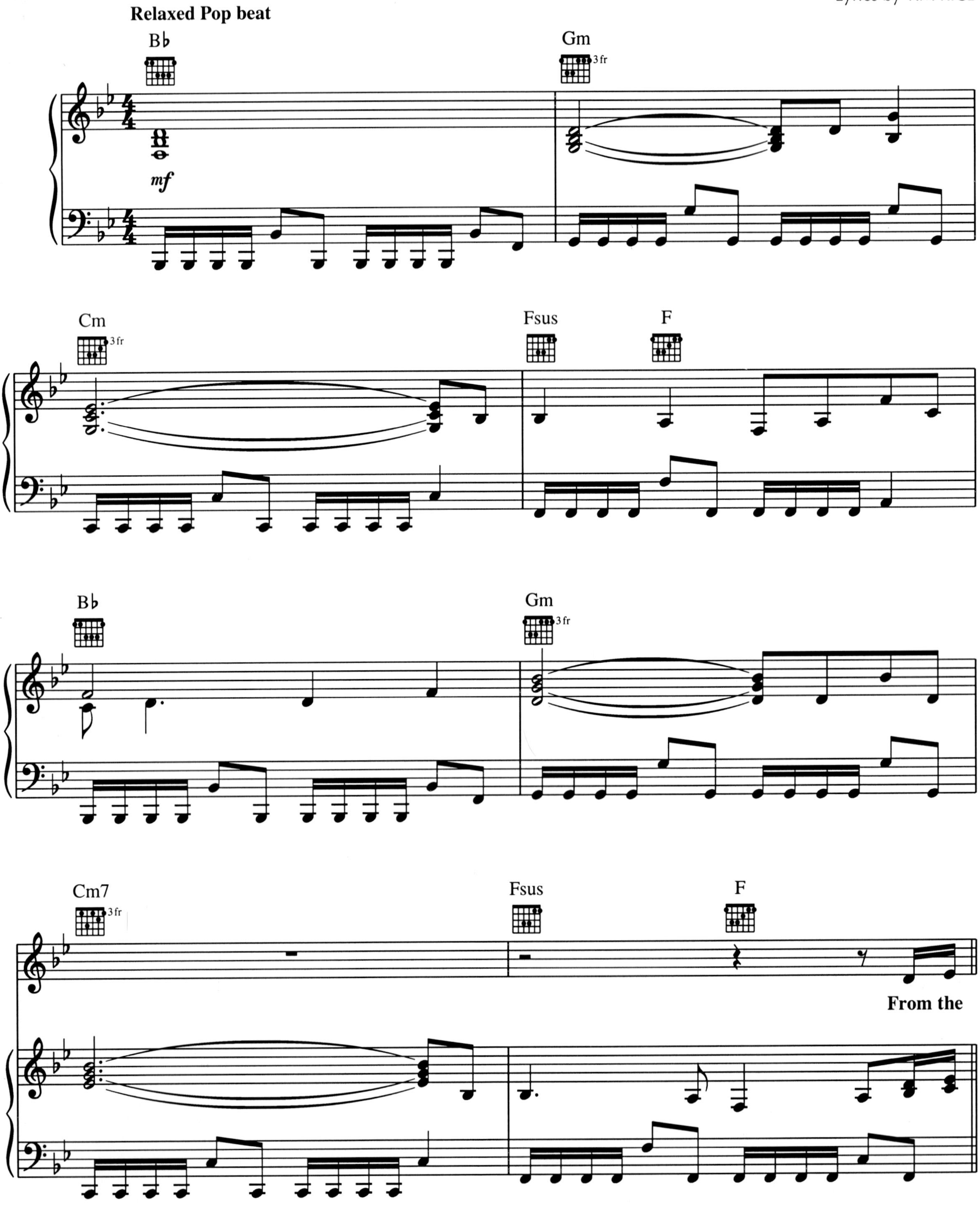

Relaxed Pop beat

From the